The rea

Bodybuilding a
of a

Courtney Smith

Global Grace
B o o k s

The real Mr Universe

Bodybuilding and Jesus Christ the greatest of all in the universe

Published by
Global Grace Books
22 Holyhead Road
Birmingham
B21 8JS
UK
globalgracebooks@gmail.com

First edition
© Copyright C. Smith 2022
ISBN 978-1-9998119-7-6
Printed in Great Britain

All rights reserved.
This book or parts thereof may not be reproduced in any form, stored in any retrieval system, or transmitted in any form by any means—electronic, mechanical, photocopy, recording, or otherwise—without prior written permission of the author.

Acknowledgements

As Christians, we believe that all of us live our lives before the face of God. The shorter Westminster catechism poses the question, "What is the chief end of man?" In other words, "What is the most important thing for us?" The answer comes back, "To glorify God and enjoy him forever." There is a saying, "The main thing is to keep the main thing, the main thing!" The main thing is to live to please the Lord. We read in the New Testament epistle to the Colossians in chapter 3:17, "And whatever you do in word or deed, do all in the name of the Lord Jesus, giving thanks to God the Father through Him." All our skills, talents and abilities are gifts given to us by God, even though we have to work hard to refine them. We are all here for a purpose. Nobody is totally useless.

This little booklet is an offering to the Lord. It is very simple and straight forward, but I hope and pray the Lord will use it to help somebody find Him and inspire some who already follow Him. I ought to have penned this a few decades ago, but I have to thank Mrs Smith, my wife Gillian, who persuaded me to get active and do this work for such a time as this.

I would also like to thank Chaplain Ray Morris for proof reading the manuscript and also Ian and Jane Walkington of Providence Chapel, Hookgate, Staffordshire for proof reading and editing the work.

Forward

The Real Mr Universe takes you on a journey of not only the writers own experience and knowledge of the history of bodybuilding, but also his own journey of the discovery of the real and ultimate MR UNIVERSE Jesus Christ.

The sport of bodybuilding requires dedication, focus, sacrifice, discipline and commitment to achieve your personal goals and outcomes. Without the afore mentioned one will never reach the heights of previous champions mentioned in this book. Courtney brilliantly tells his own personal story of how he became interested in the sport of bodybuilding and that story many young skinny teenagers can relate to. In fact, while reading his story I recollect being that skinny teenager who looked in the mirror, did a double bicep pose and realised I wanted to change the way I looked. Courtney wanted to look like the guys in the magazines and that would require firstly the building of his knowledge about the sport that would then give him the tools on his quest for becoming muscular and stronger.

Although this book details to history of body building and it's rise to becoming a global sport worth millions, at the heart of this story lies the history of Jesus Christ and Courtney's coming to put his faith in the one who was sent by God to become the ultimate sacrifice for our sins. Some might say, "What has Jesus got to do with the sport of bodybuilding?" Well, there's a well-known saying in the sport that many directly and indirectly will know and that is, "No

Pain No Gain." You see, as Courtney points out in this book Jesus did go through pain and suffering at the hand's of the brutal, ruling Roman regime 2000 years ago. Why did God allow His son to suffer a humiliating death on the cross? It was for our gain and that gain is our sins that lead to eternal death being wiped away because of His love for us.

I would encourage anyone who takes the time to read this book, to adopt an open mind, to put aside your biases or preconceived ideas and go on your own personal journey of discovery, as you learn not only about the history of bodybuilding but also the history of the real Mr Universe Jesus Christ. If you will afford the book your time I'm sure you'll enjoy and begin to question your own life's journey about faith and God.

It is stated that the richest bodybuilder of all time is none other than Arnold Schwarzenegger. His net worth is estimated to be $300 million. Many past and present bodybuilders claim Arnold to be the greatest bodybuilder of all time. As Courtney quotes Schwarzenegger states, "I was always dreaming about very powerful people. Dictators and things like that. I was always impressed by people who could be remembered for hundreds of years. Even like Jesus, being remembered for thousands of years." Schwarzenegger's may well believe he is the greatest bodybuilder of all time, that he has reached all his goals, that being fame, riches and accolades, but Schwarzenegger's achievements will never be compared to the real Mr Universe Jesus Christ. In the words of Jesus Christ, "And what do you benefit if you gain the whole world but lose your own soul?" (Mark 8:36). Only the real Mr Universe can forgive sins and grant eternal life.

As you read through this book, I pray Christ will introduce Himself to you, as He did to Courtney and millions of others worldwide.

Lance Blackwood (Pastor of Legacy Church, Walsall)

Contents

Chapter 1 Mr Universe Unequalled

Chapter 2 Mr Universe Unique

Chapter 3 Mr Universe our Saviour

Chapter 4 Mr Universe the Good News Bearer

Chapter 5 The Return of the King

Chapter 6 Mr Universe the Life Changer

Introduction

In the sport of bodybuilding, prior to the creation of the Mr Olympia competition in 1965, the top title was Mr Universe. The most muscular men from various nations compete against each other and the ones in each category voted by the judges to be the best were awarded the titles.

When you think of Mr Universe, what pictures come into your mind? An extremely big, muscular, lean and chiselled physique? Let's say you could put together the ideal or "dream physique." Twenty-two-inch arms with freakishly peaked biceps like Arnold Schwarzenegger or Robby Robinson in their heyday. Pecs (chest muscles) like Lou Ferrigno, who played the Incredible Hulk in the television series. Watermelon like deltoids (shoulder muscles) like Sergio Oliva or Dennis Tinerino. Lats ("V" shaped muscles across the back) like Lee Haney or Dorian Yates with a tiny waspish waist like Brian Buchanan had, which was reputed to be 26"and had a 30" difference between his chest and waist measurements in his prime. You could give this dream physique thighs like Tom Platz, who was affectionately known as the "Quad father" due to the size of his quadriceps thigh muscles and calves like the 1982 Mr Olympia winner Chris Dickerson and what an amazing physique you would have. You may combine all these attributes and still be nowhere close to the quality of the Mr Universe I will introduce to you. No anabolic steroids, human growth hormone, designer drugs or performance enhancing substances could ever help anybody to attain to the likeness of our Mr Universe.

His name? The Lord Jesus Christ! He is the real and ultimate Mr Universe

1. Mr Universe Unequalled

In the gospel of John chapter 1:3, we read "All things were made by Him, and without Him, nothing was made that was made." The atheists amongst us tell us that there is no God. The universe, they maintain is either eternal without beginning or it created itself. Their creed can be summed up, "In the beginning there was nothing, then nothing exploded then nothing became everything!" The Bible never seeks to prove the existence of God. God's existence is assumed. Denying God's existence, means that you believe that this orderly universe with the appearance of design, which, although no longer perfect due to the effects of sin and the curse of God, contains beauty, majesty and marvellous creatures and wonders for us to behold, came about by chance.

Consider for a moment your own eyes. We take them for granted. They are one four thousandth of our bodyweight but are the means by which we process eighty percent of the information we receive from around us. A tiny part called the retina, contains about one hundred and thirty million rod shaped cells, which detect light intensity and transmit impulses to the visual cortex of the brain by means of a million nerve fibres. Almost six million cone shaped cells do the same job but respond specifically to colour variation. Your eyes can handle half a million messages at once and are kept clear by ducts producing just the right amount of fluid with which the lids clean both eyes at once in one five hundredth of a second. Your body did not come about by chance. The universe did not come through chance. The building you may be sitting in right now did not happen by chance. It had a designer. It was purposefully built. It's obvious.

Consider the world around us. If the earth were as small as the moon, its gravitation would make human movement almost impossible. If earth were as close to the Sun as Venus, the heat would be unbearable. If it were as far away as Mars, every region would experience snow and ice nightly. If the oceans were half their size, we would get only a quarter of our present rainfall. If they were an eighth larger, the annual rainfall would increase by 400%, turning the earth into a vast uninhabitable swamp. Water freezes at 0° Centigrade but if the oceans were subject to that law, the amount of thawing in the Polar Regions would not balance out and we would all end up encased in ice. To prevent this catastrophe, God put salt in the sea to alter the freezing point. It is not the result of billions of years of blind chance. It is His handiwork.

Concerning atheism, the Bible, in Psalm 14:1 says, "The fool has said in his heart 'There is no God.'" Many, if not most people who claim to be intellectual atheists are that way because they do not want there to be a God. Behind it all is the love of sin and the desire to be free from being answerable to a God who will one day judge them for the lives they lived. Richard Dawkins was honest enough to admit it in his BBC television series "Souls of Britain" when he remarked, "I devoutly wish that we lived in a post-God society!" and listen to this frank confession by Nobel prize winning scientist George Wald, "When it comes to the origin of life on this earth, there are only two possibilities: creation or spontaneous generation (evolution). There is no third way. Spontaneous generation was disproved a hundred years ago, but that leads us to one other conclusion: that of supernatural creation. We cannot accept that on philosophical grounds, therefore, we choose to believe the impossible; that life arose spontaneously by chance." Rather than accept the obvious or go where the evidence leads, that there is a Creator, this scientist chose to believe the impossible. That is like the judge who said, "My mind is made up. Do not confuse me with the facts!"

- Mankind does not need to wonder where the universe came from or how life originated. The verse mentioned at the start of the chapter tells us. Mr Universe, Jesus Christ made "all things." In Colossians 1:16 we read, "For by Him all things were created that are on earth, visible and invisible, whether thrones or dominions...All things were created through Him and for Him." In case you did not get the message, in Hebrews 1:2, we read, "...through whom also He made the worlds." He is the life giver and the judge of us all on the day when we will be judged and have to give account for our lives. Imagine that! All of us will have to answer to Him on that day.

These are not the views of a small lunatic fringe on a par with believers in a flat earth, the tooth fairy or the spaghetti monster. Many eminent scientists and University Professors espouse the Biblical stance. Dr A.J. Monty-White has produced a documentary for BBC television, authored books and has been a senior University Administrator at the University of Wales. Stuart Burgess is a professor of engineering and helped to design the gold medal winning Olympic bicycles for the Great Britain squad in the 2012 games. At the time of writing, he is the professor at the University of Bristol and publishes his research in high-impact, peer review, scientific journals as well as authoring several books.

Professor Andy McIntosh is an emeritus Professor of Thermodynamics at the University of Leeds and an adjunct Professor at the University at Mississippi. I could give other examples of Professors and intellectuals who hold the Biblical stance, but my point is that folk who believe in the Bible are not a bunch of dunderheads who have committed intellectual suicide. The names I've quoted can be checked out and like anybody these days put to the test. Their credentials are as solid as anybody's. The Bible is like the anvil that has worn out the hammers of the sceptics over the years and will continue to do so.

When you look at Jesus, you have to marvel and look with admiration. Even the sceptic of Christianity H.G. Wells, had to admit that "Jesus Christ ....is easily the dominant figure in history." Human imagination has come up with superheroes like Superman, Batman, Spiderman, the Incredible Hulk, Ironman and I am sure you can think of a whole host of others. All these pale into insignificance in comparison with Jesus. Even if you combine all their powers into one individual. He, however, is not the product of Hollywood, Marvel or D.C. comics. Jesus did all the things that you would expect God to do if He became a human being.

If God became a human being, you would expect Him to make a dramatic entrance into the world. A completely different entrance to anybody else ever has. In the Old Testament, more than seven hundred years before Christ, the prophet Isaiah made an amazing prophecy. In Isaiah 7:14, we have the announcement that the virgin would bear a child who would be "Emmanuel", God with us.

People often scoff at the virgin birth but if you bear in mind who was being born and the kind of life he lived. If God became a human being, you would expect Him to be so wise, wiser than anybody before or since and with such wisdom that it would blow people's minds. Look at His parables, the Good Samaritan and the Prodigal son, how He answered every question fired at Him and silenced His enemies with His wisdom. On one occasion, when the authorities wanted Jesus silenced and sent men to bring Him back, they came back empty handed. When the authorities demanded to know why they did not bring Jesus back with them, all those who were sent could say was, "No one ever spoke like this man!" (John 7:46). When Jesus had finished preaching His sermon on the mount, we read in Matthew 7:28, 29 "...that the people were astonished at His teaching, for He taught them as one having authority, and not as the scribes."

If God became a human being, you would expect Him to do things which would be impossible for ordinary mere mortals to do. I encourage you to read the Gospels. Look at the signs and wonders Jesus performed. His enemies do not deny that He performed them, they simply said that He performed these amazing deeds by the power of the devil, or Beelzebub.

In the Gospels, Jesus is constantly telling people to do things which are impossible for them to do. For instance:

- He said to a man who was paralysed, "Rise up and walk" and the man does so. (Luke 5:23).
- He said to a man with a withered hand, "Stretch out your hand" and the man does so (Matthew 12:13).
- He said to a man who was born blind, "Go to the pool of Siloam and wash". The man does so and came back seeing (John 9:7).
- He said to a man with leprosy, "Be cleansed!" The man was instantaneously healed (Mark 1:41).

If a good friend of mine died and was buried, I could go to his grave four days later and order him to come out. And do you know what would happen? Nothing! I would stand there looking even more foolish than I really am. Not so Jesus. He went to the grave of His friend Lazarus, who had been dead and buried for four days, and said, "Lazarus come out."

Lazarus rose up and came out alive. Bible commentators have said that if Jesus had not have said, 'Lazarus come out!", then all the dead would have come out alive from their graves that day.

If God became a human being, you would expect Him to make a dramatic exit from the world, just as remarkable and memorable as His entrance. In the New Testament book of Acts chapter 1:9-11, we have the narrative of the Ascension of Jesus where He returns to heaven in front of a crowd. "Now when He had spoken these things, while they watched He was taken up, and a cloud received Him out of their sight. And while they looked steadfastly toward heaven as He went up, behold, two men stood by them in white apparel, who also said, "Men of Galilee, why do you stand gazing into heaven? This same Jesus, who was taken up from you into heaven, will so come in like manner as you saw Him go into heaven."

So, Jesus Christ is Mr Universe unequalled. I will finish this first chapter with a poem by James Allen Francis called "One solitary life."

> "He was born in an obscure village, the child of a peasant. He grew up in another village, where He worked in a carpenter shop until He was 30. Then for three years, He was an itinerant preacher.
>
> He never wrote a book. He never held an office. He never had a family or owned a home. He did not go to college. He never lived in a big city. He never travelled 200 miles from the place where He was born. He did

none of the things that usually accompany greatness. He had no credentials but Himself.

He was only 33 when the tide of public opinion turned against Him. His friends ran away. One of them denied Him. He was turned over to His enemies and went through the mockery of a trial. He was nailed to a cross between two thieves. While He was dying, His executioners gambled for His garments, the only property He had on earth. When He was dead, He was laid in a borrowed grave through the pity of a friend.

Twenty centuries have come and gone, and today He is the central figure of the human race. I am well within the mark when I say that all the armies that ever marched, all the navies that ever sailed, all the parliaments that ever sat, all the kings that ever reigned have not affected the life of man on this earth as much as that One solitary life "

2. Mr Universe Unique

"I was always dreaming about very powerful people, dictators and things like that. I was just always impressed by people who could be remembered for hundreds of years, or even like Jesus, being remembered for thousands of years." - Arnold Schwarzenegger

The above quote by Arnold Schwarzenegger is from the 1970s bodybuilding movie "Pumping Iron", which is the story of the 1975 Mr Olympia and Mr Universe contests in Pretoria, South Africa, is a classic, which brought popularity to the sport in the 1970's.

Jesus Christ is not remembered for thousands of years without good reason. It's a point of great contention but many consider the seven-time Mr Olympia winner Arnold Schwarzenegger the greatest bodybuilder of all time. He is over seventy years old now, no longer has that prize winning physique and even had to undergo cardiac surgery in the 1990s to correct a defective valve. Muhammad Ali (A.K.A. Cassius Clay) was very keen on telling anybody who would listen that he was the greatest heavyweight boxer of all time. He was the first heavyweight to win the World title three times. In 1964 he beat Charles "Sonny" Liston, in 1974 he beat George Foreman in the 'Rumble in the jungle' in Kinshasa and then in 1978 he regained the title he had previously lost against Leon Spinks. After Ali retired, He was afflicted with

Parkinson's disease which resulted in the "Louisville lip" being silenced and those famous dancing feet reduced to a slow shuffle. He sadly departed this mortal coil on 3rd June 2016 aged 74. The best of the best die.

There is an old saying, "the best of men are at best, men!" The question is, was Jesus Christ the same as the rest of us? When He died, did He stay dead?

The Christian faith stands or falls with the resurrection of Jesus Christ from the dead. If you take away the resurrection of Christ, there is no Christianity. If you take away the resurrection of Christ, you take away the foundation of the Christian faith. If Jesus Christ did not rise from the dead, then Christians have been taken for a ride and are the victims of the biggest hoax in the history of mankind, if Jesus Christ is still dead.

In 1984, there was a Bishop of Durham named David Jenkins, not to be confused with the Scottish 400 metres runner of the same name. He caused much consternation at the time when he announced that he did not believe in the resurrection of Christ. The phrase he used to describe the resurrection was that "it was a conjuring trick with bones." Also in the news headlines was the fact that he was ordained in York Minster, which, soon after the ordination, was struck by a bolt of lightning which resulted in a fire which gutted the building.

Did Jesus really rise from the dead? In the Old Testament book of Job, chapter 14:14, we have a question that people have asked all down the ages and in every place, "If a man die, will he live again?" We know that when it comes to death, there are no "ifs". Worldwide, almost 2 people die every second. Every minute, approximately 105 people die. Hourly, approximately 6,316 people die and approximately 151,600 people die daily which equates to 55.3 million people who die annually. I heard of an undertaker who would sign his letters, "Yours eventually!" We know from our experience as human beings that when anybody or anything dies, they tend to stay dead. Was this the same with Jesus Christ? Not according to the Christian faith. The very first Christians proclaimed that Jesus died, yes, He died, and that very publicly, that is, in front of a crowd. He was buried and after three days, He rose physically from the grave (1 Corinthians 15:1-3).

All parties, believers and unbelievers alike, agree with the fact that the tomb which contained the body of Jesus was empty three days later. The matter on which they disagree is, what happened to the body of Jesus? I read the account of a rationalist unbelieving lawyer who wanted to disprove Christianity. His point of attack was the resurrection of Christ, because Christianity would be sunk if Christ did not rise from the dead. The conclusion was not what Frank Morris expected. The evidence led to the publication of the masterpiece defending the resurrection of Christ. The book, "Who moved the stone?" is well worth a read.

Some sceptics claim that it was the authorities, be it Roman or Jewish who removed the body of Jesus. If that were the case, then when the first Christians began telling the world that Christ was risen from the dead, all that the authorities needed to do to stop the Christian faith and "nip it in the bud", would have been to produce the body and say, "Here's your 'risen saviour!'"

Other sceptics allege that the disciples stole the body of Jesus. Observe these facts; the authorities had set a guard at the tomb. The account of that is at the end of the twenty seventh chapter of the Gospel of Matthew. Secondly the disciples were a cowardly group of individuals who ran off and left Jesus all alone in the hour of His greatest need when He was arrested in the garden of Gethsemane. But we observe later how these disciples suffered and died for unflinchingly proclaiming the resurrection of Christ.

Some cynics who read the Gospels, dispute the fact that Jesus really did die on the cross on that first "Good Friday." They maintain that Jesus merely swooned and his ignorant disciples assumed He was dead. They say the Roman soldiers were not medical experts and only had a primitive understanding of the human anatomy and medicine which mistakenly led them to believe that Jesus was dead.

It is true, that while the Roman soldiers were not doctors, they were fairly efficient at killing people. It is what they did with expertise. They likely put people to death on a daily basis. At least three on this particular Friday. If a Roman soldier lost a prisoner, that indiscretion would cost him his life. That is why, in Acts 16, the Philippian jailer was about to kill himself when the earthquake caused the prisoners to be loosed. The Romans made sure that Jesus was really dead because, in the gospel of John 19:34 we read that the soldier pierced Jesus' side with a spear which caused "blood and water"(blood and plasma) to come out, which only occurs after death. It was likely that Jesus' pericardium, which is a sack of fluid around the heart, was pierced. If you think about it, a half dead Jesus, who was badly injured from the flogging which He received and being hanged on a cross for at least six hours, in need of medical treatment and food, would be unlikely to push away the stone from the tomb, overpower the armed soldiers, stagger to the city then convince His disciples that He was the glorious Prince of life. It is amazing the lengths that people go to, to deny the resurrection of Christ. It makes sense to believe in the resurrection of Christ for many reasons, but we will look at four:

- The Old Testament predicted it.
- Jesus Himself predicted it.
- The disciples were transformed.
- People are transformed today.

The resurrection of Christ is an historic fact. It was part of God's plan from before the foundation of the world as part of the plan for the salvation of a lost and sinful mankind.

In Luke 24, after His resurrection, Jesus appeared to His disciples. He gave them convincing proof that He was not a ghost or a hallucination. He even ate a piece of fish and a honeycomb for them (v41-43). He then opened their minds so they could understand the scriptures and said "...all things must be fulfilled that is written about Me in the Law of Moses, the prophets and the Psalms." (Luke 24:44). He continued to say, "This is what is written. The Christ will suffer and rise from the dead on the third day" (v46). So, there is a sense in which none of us will understand the scriptures unless Jesus opens our understanding. Let us pray that our minds are not kept from understanding the scriptures as is the case with many.

Also in the same chapter, after His resurrection, there is the account when Jesus was walking on the road from Jerusalem to Emmaus. Two disciples, one named Cleopas and the other unnamed, were having a conversation with Jesus whom they did not recognise. In Luke 24:25-27 we read, "Then He said to them, 'O foolish ones, and slow of heart to believe in all that the prophets have spoken! Ought not the Christ to have suffered these things and to enter into His glory?' And beginning at Moses and all the Prophets, He expounded to them in all the Scriptures the things concerning Himself."

On the day of Pentecost, when the Apostle Peter preached to the multitudes in Jerusalem, He quotes from Psalm 16:8-11 as a "proof text" to his fellow Jews, for the resurrection of Christ. He teaches them that this Psalm is prophetic or a "Messianic" Psalm. It is about Christ (literally, the Messiah or Anointed). The author of the Psalm was king David of Israel who died nearly a thousand years before Christ. Peter reminds his hearers that David's tomb was there in

Jerusalem for them all to see. Verse 10 of the Psalm makes it clear that the Psalm could not be about David because David had died and like everyone else, his body had decomposed, or in the words of the Psalm seen "corruption", which the "holy one" written about in the Psalm would not experience. Peter preaches that David was writing prophetically about the Messiah. Christ went to the grave, but He never saw decay or corruption. Unlike the rest of the human race, Jesus did not decay because, by His resurrection, He fulfilled Psalm 16.

Psalm 22 is another prophetic or Messianic Psalm. It's about the suffering, death, burial and resurrection of the One who cries out, "My God, my God, why have you forsaken me?" (22:1). In verses 7-8, the forsaken One is mocked by onlookers. In the v16, His hands and feet are pierced and in v18, His clothes are gambled for, whilst in v15, He goes down to the dust of death. Despite going down to the dust of death, He is rescued. He emerges triumphantly and praises the Lord amongst the congregation and all the ends of the earth will turn to the Lord (vs27-31). If you read the accounts of the crucifixion, death, burial and resurrection in Matthew chapters 27 and 28, Mark chapters 15 and 16 and Luke chapters 23 and 24, you will see how Psalm 22 was fulfilled literally. The events of the crucifixion of Christ are so clear in Psalm 22 that the early church referred to it as the *Fifth Gospel*.

Another Old Testament passage that predicts Jesus' death and resurrection is one that is often referred to as the "Suffering Servant" passage in Isaiah 52:13 - 53:12. We must keep in mind that this passage is from over seven hundred years before the events happened, which makes it all the more amazing. It is so clearly about Christ, that it is incredible that every Old Testament believing individual has not accepted Jesus (or Yeshua) as the Messiah and fulfilment of the prophetic expectations. Here is the passage,

> "Behold, My Servant shall deal very prudently;
> He shall be exalted and be very high.
> Just as many were astonished at you
> So His visage (face) was marred more than any man,
> And His form more than the sons of men;
> So shall He sprinkle many nations.
> Kings shall shut their mouths at Him;
> For what had not been told them they shall see,
> And what they had not heard they shall consider.
> Who has believed our report?
> And to whom has the arm of the LORD been revealed?
> For He shall grow up before Him as a tender plant,
> And as a root out of dry ground.
> He has no form or comeliness;
> And when we see Him,
> There is no beauty that we should desire Him.
> He is despised and rejected by men,
> A man of sorrows and acquainted with grief.

And we hid, as it were, our faces from Him.

Surely He has borne our griefs

And carried our sorrows;

Yet we esteemed Him stricken,

Smitten by God and afflicted.

But He was wounded for our transgressions (literally when we overstep the mark and break God's will for us),

He was bruised for our iniquities (wrongdoings);

The chastisement (punishment) for our peace was upon Him, And by His stripes (whiplashes) we are healed.

All we like sheep have gone astray;

We have turned everyone to his own way;

And the LORD has laid on Him the iniquity of us all,

He was oppressed and He was afflicted,

Yet He opened not His mouth;

He was led as a lamb to the slaughter,

And as a sheep before its shearers is silent,

So He opened not His mouth.

He was taken from prison and from judgement

And who will declare His generation?

For He was cut off from the land of the living;

For the transgressions of My people He was stricken

And they made His grave with the wicked

> But with the rich at His death,
>
> Because He had done no violence,
>
> Nor was any deceit in His mouth.
>
> Yet it pleased the LORD to bruise Him;
>
> He has put Him to grief.
>
> When You make His soul an offering for sin,
>
> He shall see His seed; He shall prolong His days,
>
> And the pleasure of the LORD shall prosper in His hand.
>
> He shall see the labour of His soul, and be satisfied.
>
> By His knowledge My righteous Servant shall justify many,
>
> For He shall bear their iniquities.
>
> Therefore I will divide Him a portion with the strong,
>
> Because He poured out His soul unto death,
>
> And He was numbered with the transgressors,
>
> And He bore the sin of many,
>
> And made intercession for the transgressors."

The passage is absolutely packed or "stacked," as some would say but for times' sake, we will consider a few points. Look at all His sufferings and remember, this passage is from more than seven hundred years before Christ came, but it reads as though it is from the Gospels. Why did the "Suffering One" go through it all? It was to save, or rescue lost and erring sinners.

Look at verse 11 where we are told that "He shall see the labour of His soul and be satisfied," and, in verse 10, "He shall see His seed, He shall prolong His days." That is the resurrection. After all the suffering and pouring "out His soul unto death," He emerges triumphantly.

As well as the Old Testament scriptures:

(i) Jesus Himself Predicted it.

In the point above, I quoted from Luke 24 from the narrative of Jesus, on the road to Emmaus speaking with two sceptical disciples. In Luke 24:44, Jesus said, "This is what I told you while I was still with you."

In Matthew 16:23 we read, "From that time on Jesus began to explain to His disciples that He must go to Jerusalem and suffer many things at the hands of the elders, Chief Priests and the teachers of the law, and that He must be killed and on the third day be raised to life."

In Matthew 17:22, 23 we read, "When they came together in Galilee, He said to them, 'The Son of Man is going to be betrayed into the hands of man. They will kill Him, and on the third day, He will be raised to life.' "

In Matthew 27:63 we read that the chief priests and Pharisees said to Pontius Pilate, "Sir, we remember while He was still alive, how that deceiver said, "After three days I will rise!'", then Pilate gave the order for the tomb to be made secure until the third day. So, Jesus on at least three occasions during His ministry predicted His suffering, death and resurrection.

(ii) The disciples were transformed.

These men who had faithfully followed Jesus for over three years were a bunch of cowards, who, when it came to the crunch, ran off and left Jesus all alone to save their own skins. On the night of the betrayal and arrest, Peter denied three times that he knew Jesus. Of the disciples, in Mark 14:50, we read, "And they all forsook Him and fled."

What was it that caused this bunch of cowards to become fearless men who "turned the world upside down?" What happened to cause them to give their lives proclaiming that Jesus died and rose from the dead? People will not die for something they know is not true. If you could save your life, when under threat, you would do. Yet, not one of the Apostles denied the truth of the resurrection because they saw the Risen Christ.

Here are a few examples.

- James the son of Zebedee, was killed by the sword of Herod Agrippa. (Acts 12:1-19).
- The first century Jewish historian Flavius Josephus (AD 37-100) informs us that James, the half-brother of Jesus was thrown down from the temple and when he would not die was clubbed to death.
- Peter was crucified upside down in Rome.

- The Apostle Paul was beheaded in Rome under the Emperor Nero Caesar.
- Sources from the Apostolic period inform us that all the disciples suffered martyrdom except John the son of Zebedee, who was tortured and when he would not die, was banished to the isle of Patmos, where he was not expected to be heard from again. Whilst he was there, Jesus spoke to him and revealed to him the book of Revelation. There have been many martyrs down the ages for many different causes and there still are today. The key difference is that the Apostles were eyewitnesses of the truth they proclaimed.

These all proclaimed the truth that Jesus is risen.

(ii) People are still transformed

Saul of Tarsus was from the strictest party in first century Judaism. He was a Pharisee. He was so zealous for his religion that he hated Christians. He voted against them when he was a Sanhedrin member, pursued them to foreign cities. When Stephen became the first Christian martyr, Saul approved of his death and those doing the stoning of Stephen to death, laid their cloaks at his feet. What was it that caused this zealot to do a hundred and eighty degree turn and become the greatest missionary and evangelist of the Christian faith in all of history?

The Damascus Road experience has become a cliché in the English language but that was when Saul was stopped in his tracks by the Risen Lord whilst on another "Christian hunting" expedition. Jesus, whom he considered to be an imposter and false Messiah, appeared to Saul and changed the history of the world. You can read that in Acts chapters 9, 22 and 26. To this day, multitudes of men, women, boys and girls can testify of how the same Risen Christ has changed their lives and set them free from enslaving habits. Jesus said, in John 8:36, "If the Son makes you free, you shall be free indeed!"

I began the chapter with a quote by Arnold Schwarzenegger from the film "Pumping Iron." It is not without good reason that Jesus Christ is "remembered for thousands of years!" The resurrection of Christ testifies to His identity.

By His resurrection, He answers those sceptics who say, "If somebody came back from the dead and told me what it was like, then I would believe in life after death!" He did it.

Jesus Christ is the Unique Mr Universe.

3. Mr Universe Our Saviour

In the first chapter, I made mention of judgement day. It is the day when we will all have to give account for our lives before God. Speaking of the day of judgement, both the Old Testament predicted it in the book of Daniel and in the last book of the Bible Revelation. Both read, "And the books were opened," (Daniel 7:10, Revelation 20:12).

Judgement day is a problem for us because every human being is guilty of what the Bible calls sin. There are several descriptions of sin in the Bible. One is falling short and another is transgressing or overstepping the mark. Sin is an overwhelming theme in the Bible - right from the earliest chapters of its pages in the book of Genesis, right through to the closing chapters of the final book, the book of Revelation. Sin separates us from God. Sin condemns us before God because He is a pure, holy and just God who cannot have sin in His presence.

A few years ago, The National Geographic channel aired a documentary on the search for Adam. Dr Spencer Wells undertook what was known as "the geographic project." DNA samples were taken from adult males from every corner of the globe. Spencer Wells' research demonstrated that all males on earth have the same male ancestor because we all have the same genetic mutation of the "Y" chromosome. When National Geographic tells us that we all have the same male ancestor, the attitude of the world is, "Wow, how profound and amazing. This is earth shattering news!" But when the Bible tells us that we all have the same set of parents, the reaction by the world is not so charitable. Most of us who have been Christians for any amount of time have heard the early chapters of the Bible being dismissed as myths, fairy tales, and parables or symbolic.

The Bible teaches that all humans are descendants of Adam and Eve, who were created by God. Jesus Himself reiterates this in the New Testament. The Bible teaches that the sin of Adam and Eve and its resulting consequences have passed down to all their descendants, which is us (Romans 5:12). Sin causes death, chaos, natural disasters, crime, anti-social behaviour and all the horrible things we see in the world. You might not have committed adultery or fornication but according to Jesus, if you looked with lustful desire at another person you are just as guilty. You might not have murdered anybody but if you have been angry enough in your thoughts, you are just as guilty. In the Sermon on the Mount, the standard Jesus sets before us shows us how far short we fall of God's requirements of us (Matthew 5:20-48). If you were dangling over a cliff by a chain made of ten links, it takes only one link to break which would cause you to plunge to your death. We read in the Epistle of James, "For whoever shall keep the whole law, and yet stumble in one point, he is guilty of all." (James 2:10).

Sin has tragic consequences in daily life. A poll from the UK in August 2019 revealed that 89%, that is, virtually 9 out of 10 young people aged 16-29, believe that their lives had no meaning or purpose. How sad! Half of UK residents questioned claimed to be Atheist. Church attendance was down to less than 4.5%. The study found that 30% of these young people said they were "stuck in a rut" and 84% didn't believe they were "living their best life." All caused by sin and the rejection of God.

If our media, be it television documentaries, schools, colleges, universities, radio, books and magazines continue banging the drum, "we've come from nothing, are going to nothing and are answerable to nobody," society had better be prepared for what comes with such notions. Atheists and evolutionists tell us that we are on a par with the beasts and when we behave in a manner which the Bible calls sinful, it is simply us doing what our DNA dictates. The God denying evolutionist Richard Dawkins, in his book, "River out of Eden," writes, "The universe we observe has....no design, no purpose, no evil and no good, nothing but blind, pitiful indifference...DNA neither knows nor cares. DNA just is. And we dance to its music."

The secular world tells us that we are on the level of the apes. The Bible teaches that that we are created in the image of God, and Jesus says in Matthew 12:12, "Of how much more value then is a man than a sheep?" and in Matthew 10:31,"...You are of more value than many sparrows." It is small wonder that crime, anti-social behaviour, fear, anxiety and lack of respect are on the rise since God has been kicked out of society!

Mr Universe made you. You do not need to wonder where we came from. He made you to live for Him. Life has a purpose? Do you know it? Sin blinds us to reality. Mr Universe Jesus Christ said, He came to give "...recovery of sight to the blind" (Luke 4:18). Sin imprisons. Mr Universe Jesus Christ said He came "to set at liberty those who are oppressed" (Luke 4:18). Sin kills. Mr Universe Jesus Christ said He came that you "may have life, and that...more abundantly" (John 10:10).

On one occasion in the Gospels, Jesus, even though He was in the world and could have had people serving Him said that He, "...did not come to be served but to serve and give His life as a ransom for many." The word for "ransom" in the original language is the word "lutron" which is literally, "unloose," and is used for the price to set free a captive or hostage. Sinful mankind can no more set himself free from sin than a man can lift himself off the ground by his own boot laces. If you are from an English-speaking country, you are likely to know the nursery rhyme of Humpty Dumpty.

> "Humpty Dumpty sat on the wall.
>
> Humpty Dumpty had a great fall,
>
> All the king's horses and all the king's men,
>
> Couldn't put Humpty together again."

This nursery rhyme is a good analogy of the Gospel. Man was created by God whole and good. We were intact and in a right relationship with God and could communicate with Him without any barriers between us. Then came the incident that theologians call "the fall." This is when sin came into the world and ruined everything. Death, sickness, strife, and broken relationships entered in. The relationship between man and God, man and man and man and his environment was ruined beyond repair, humanly speaking. That is Humpty Dumpty's fall. We try many things such as education, healthcare, politics, counselling, the arts, sport and even religion in an effort to "fix" man. "All the king's horses and all the king's men, couldn't put Humpty together again."

Where "All the king's horses and all the king's men" failed, that is where Jesus, as it were, steps in. In John 8:34 Jesus says that "Whoever commits sin is the slave of sin." That is why we see so many broken New Year's resolutions. We are enslaved to sin, unable to free ourselves. The word for slave in that verse from John 8:34 is literally, a person in shackles or chains unable to free themselves. A couple of verses later, in John 8:36, Jesus says, "If the Son sets you free, you will be free indeed!" In John 19:30, as Jesus was hanging on the cross at Calvary, He cried out, "It is finished!" Three words in English but one word in the original New Testament. The word means "fully paid." There is a hymn which contains the words, "Jesus paid it all,"

> All to Him I owe,
> Sin had left its crimson stain,
> He washed it white as snow."

We will look a bit more at what Jesus did in our next chapter.

4. Mr Universe the Good News Bearer

Back in the days when there were muscle building adverts in magazines, there were adverts with a photograph of a big beefy muscle man with the slogan, "You too could have a body like his!" I remember when I was in my teens and first started training. I was under the impression that when you start training with weights and built your muscles, they were there to stay. I was devastated when I read that there was such a thing as muscle atrophy. That is basically "use it or lose it!" If you do not keep training, your muscles will shrink through under use or if you get injured and if you have a limb encased in plaster of paris, when it is removed, the muscles beneath it waste. That is atrophy. It takes hard graft to build muscles. It is not for the lazy. "No pain, no gain!" God has designed the human body to be active.

The good news is, that those who trust in Jesus Christ are forgiven of all their sins. 1 John 1:9 reads, "If we confess our sins, He is faithful and just to forgive us our sins and to cleanse us from all unrighteousness." We confess when we agree with God that we are sinners and ask Him to forgive us. This verse assures us that when we do so, we will be forgiven. In this life, our bodies, even the most muscular, athletic and sporty, are subject to aging, decaying, atrophy, sickness and death. In the Epistle to the Philippians 3:20-21, writing to believers, we read, "For our citizenship is in heaven, from which we also eagerly wait for the Saviour, the Lord Jesus

Christ, who will transform our lowly body that it may be conformed to His glorious body, according to the working by which He is able even to subdue all things to Himself."

Those old muscle adverts did not tell you about all the hard training, the drugs, the sleep and disciplined diet needed to build that special body. They only showed you the end results. Even the best physiques get old, succumb to illness, start to lose condition and sooner or later, dies. In order to attain a glorious body like Mr Universe, the Lord Jesus Christ, there is no need to go to a gym to train. No drugs are required. There is no need for a special diet or a rigorous lifestyle. It is by grace alone, by faith alone in Christ alone.

In 1 Timothy 4:7-8 we read, "...exercise yourself toward godliness. For bodily exercise profits a little, but godliness is profitable for all things, having promise of the life that is now and of the life which is to come." This tells us that it is good to stay in shape - healthy body and healthy mind. As we age, our hormone levels start to taper off and as we approach middle age and old age, in men and women, it starts to become noticeable that we lose muscle size and gain more body fat. Doing weight training, along with a balanced eating plan, helps to offset this. Weight training because of the nature of it and the resistance of the weights, work upon the joints to help keep the bones strong as age tends to reduce bone density. There's an old saying, "If you don't make time for exercise, you will have to make time for illness!"

There are many things beyond our control. Our times are in God's hands. The 18th century, English preacher George Whitfield said, "I am immortal till my work is done!" But there are things that we can do to help ourselves. Keeping yourself healthy can manage blood pressure, cholesterol levels; reduce the risks of diabetes, heart attacks, strokes, obesity, osteoarthritis and many other preventable health issues. Being fitter and healthier increases one's stamina and capacity for work. In Biblical days there was no public transport, television, supermarkets, restaurants, takeaways or junk food. People walked to places and had to do manual work, even to eat their meals, wash their clothes or look after their animals. They would have been naturally fitter than most people today where food is easy to get and places easier to get to. The environment would not have been polluted due to smoke. So, bodily exercise does profit a little, as 1 Timothy 4:7 says. The word for "exercise" in that passage is actually the word from which we get "gymnasium."

However, even more importantly than looking after a physical health, the Biblical text informs us that godliness is far more important because it matters now and for eternity. The body matters, it is what God gave us and as we read in the Epistle to the 1 Corinthians 6:19, "...your body is the temple of the Holy Spirit who is in you, whom you have from God, and you are not your own." We are to use our bodies to honour God in the way we live. When these bodies have grown old and gone back to the dust from whence we were taken in the beginning, the Gospels make clear that we all have to answer to our Maker.

The Lord Jesus Christ is the friend of sinners and is sometimes pictured as, "gentle Jesus, meek and mild!" The C.S. Lewis's book, "The Lion, the Witch and the Wardrobe," in one scene, it is said, "Aslan is not safe." He was a lion who was friendly and approachable, but, a lion nonetheless. Jesus welcomes all who come to Him, but we should keep in mind that in the Gospels, He spoke more about hell than He did about heaven. "He delivers us from the wrath to come" (1 Thessalonians 1:10). He said, "For the Son of Man has come to seek and to save that which was lost"(Luke 19:10). If you do not know where you are heading after this life is over, come to Him. It is not presumptuous to believe that you are saved. By no means. It is indeed in the message of the Gospel that we can have assurance. We read in 1 John 5:13, "These things I have written to you who believe in the name of the Son of God, that you may know that you have "eternal life."

A useful modern picture helps us to see what Jesus did for us by coming into the world.

The Long Silence

> "At the end of time, billions of people were seated on a great plain before God's throne. Most shrank back from the brilliant light before them. But some groups near the front talked heatedly, not cringing with shame - but with belligerence.

"Can God judge us? How can He know about suffering?" snapped a pert young brunette. She ripped open a sleeve to reveal a tattooed number from a Nazi concentration camp. "We endured terror ... beatings ... torture ... death!"

In another group a Negro boy lowered his collar. "What about this?" he demanded, showing an ugly rope burn. "Lynched, for no crime but being black!"

In another crowd there was a pregnant schoolgirl with sullen eyes: "Why should I suffer?" she murmured. "It wasn't my fault." Far out across the plain were hundreds of such groups. Each had a complaint against God for the evil and suffering He had permitted in His world.

How lucky God was to live in Heaven, where all was sweetness and light. Where there was no weeping or fear, no hunger or hatred. What did God know of all that man had been forced to endure in this world? For God leads a pretty sheltered life, they said.

So each of these groups sent forth their leader, chosen because he had suffered the most. A Jew, a Negro, a person from Hiroshima, a horribly deformed arthritic, a thalidomide child. In the centre of the vast plain, they consulted with each other. At last they were ready to present their case. It was rather clever.

Before God could be qualified to be their judge, He must endure what they had endured. Their decision was that God should be sentenced to live on earth as a man.

Let him be born a Jew. Let the legitimacy of his birth be doubted. Give him a work so difficult that even his family will think him out of his mind. Let him be betrayed by his closest friends. Let him face false charges, be tried by a prejudiced jury and convicted by a cowardly judge. Let him be tortured.

At the last, let him see what it means to be terribly alone. Then let him die so there can be no doubt he died. Let there be a great host of witnesses to verify it. As each leader announced his portion of the sentence, loud murmurs of approval went up from the throng of people assembled. When the last had finished pronouncing sentence, there was a long silence. No one uttered a word. No one moved. For suddenly, all knew that God had already served His sentence."

Anon (written before summer 1982).

His pain was our gain!

5. The Return of the King

In 1980 Arnold Schwarzenegger made a comeback in the Mr Olympia competition in Sydney, Australia. Schwarzenegger's last competitive appearance prior to this was at the 1975 Mr Olympia in Pretoria, South Africa, which was the subject of the documentary, "Pumping Iron." Schwarzenegger had won that competition to complete a run of six successive victories at the Mr Olympia contest. He had been unbeaten in Olympias since winning his first title in 1970.

Arnold Schwarzenegger was a surprise late entrant and was putting his head on the block against a whole host of strong opposition. His opponents would include the winner of the previous three competitions, Frank Zane, Boyer Coe, Chris Dickerson, Dennis Tinerino (whom I met in March of 1980, but more of that in the final chapter), Mike Mentzer, Roy Callender, Roger Walker and Roy Duval.

I would also meet Mike Mentzer at a seminar at Colton Hills School, Wolverhampton in November 1980, when he toured the UK after the competition, when feelings were still running high after a very controversial victory for Schwarzenegger. Mentzer appeared to be somewhat bitter and resentful towards Schwarzenegger, Joe Weider and the IFBB (the international federation of bodybuilders) months after the competition. In those days there was no internet so sometimes it took days or weeks for the results of overseas competitions to reach us, and we had to wait for the publication of magazines to find out the results.

I remember ringing round the magazines to find out who won the 1980 Mr Olympia.

I rang the Health and Strength and the Bodybuilding Monthly magazines, and I think it may have been the EFBB that I eventually got through to on the telephone and discovered who won. I remember a woman with a very strong south Wales accent answering the phone. I asked her, "Who won the 1980 Olympia?" "Arnold!" she replied "Arnold who?" I answered. I said that because none of us knew Arnold Schwarzenegger was competing although we obviously knew who Arnold was.

I remember acquiring a free VHS copy the documentary of "The Comeback" documentary, mentioned at the start of the chapter when buying a tub of Weider "Mega Mass 2000," weight gaining powder in the early 1990s. Arnold Schwarzenegger was widely known as the "Austrian Oak" and considered by many as the "king of bodybuilding." The 1980 Mr Olympia competition was considered by many as, "the return of the king!"

Well, the Bible has a lot to say about the return of the king. The king I am referring to is not Arnold Schwarzenegger, Lee Haney, Ronnie Coleman, Jay Cutler, Phil Heath, Sergio Oliva or any other champion bodybuilder. The king the Bible is referring to is Jesus Christ. In the New Testament, the return of the King, Jesus Christ is a dominant theme.

The New Testament teaches that the King's return will be personal. In 1 Thessalonians 4:14 we read, "The Lord Himself will descend from heaven." I, like many of you, have spoken to members of the Jehovah's Witness group. They claim they believe the Bible, but deny the personal return of Jesus and say that He returned invisibly in 1914.

This is clearly wide of the mark because in Revelation 1:7, we read, "Behold, He is coming with clouds, and every eye shall see Him, even they who pierced Him. And all the tribes of the earth will mourn because of Him." So, His return will not only be for the eyes of believers but even those who rejected him and have not accepted Him as their Lord and Saviour. In the first chapter of the book of the Acts of the Apostles, we have the account of the ascension of Jesus into heaven after His resurrection.

His first coming, or advent was literal and visible. His second advent will also be literal and visible. In Acts 1:11, we read, "This same Jesus, who was taken up from you into heaven, will so come in like manner as you saw Him go into heaven." I Thessalonians 4:16 tells us that the second advent will be a very loud, heralded event for all to see and hear because we read, "For the Lord Himself will descend from heaven with a shout, with the voice of an archangel, and with the trumpet of God". His return will be sudden and unexpected. It was first Jesus Himself who taught it. We read in a passage often referred to as the Olivet discourse, due to the location of the conversation, "Therefore you also be ready for the Son of Man is coming at an hour you do not expect." (Matthew 24:44)

In Mark 13:33 it tells us to "Take heed, watch and pray; for you do not know when the time is" and in Luke 21:35, Jesus said His return would, "come as a snare on all those who dwell on the face of the whole earth." There is so much ignorance in the world concerning the second advent of Christ that it is surely only a question of time before Jesus's words are fulfilled.

Whilst in His first advent, Jesus came in the body of His humiliation, when He came to give His life to redeem sinners. His second advent will be totally the opposite. The first time, He "took the form of a servant", when He returns "every knee shall bow to Him" (Philippians 2:5-11), which always reminds me of the hymn we sang at school assembly, "At the name of Jesus, every knee shall bow, every tongue confess Him, king of glory now!" He entered into the world, the first time as a helpless babe, the next time, it will be as the "king of kings and Lord of Lords" and "conquering lion of the tribe of Judah."

The return of Christ is described as "the blessed hope" of the believer in Titus 2:13, because it will be the culmination of history and the fulfilment of all the Old and New Testament predictions. In a previous chapter, I quoted the Apostle Paul from Philippians 3:20-21 where we read, "For our citizenship is in heaven, from which we also eagerly await for the Saviour, the Lord Jesus Christ, who will transform our lowly body that it may be conformed to His glorious body by which He is able even to subdue all things to Himself." Our lives in this world are short and uncertain in the context of eternity, even for the few who live to be over a hundred years of age. When we reach a certain age, we seem to suffer bereavement after bereavement on an increasing scale. Even the great Arnold Schwarzenegger's physique became a shadow of what it was in his pomp. His 1980 return to the Mr Olympia stage resulted in a controversial win because he was, in the view of many, a shadow of the champion he was in 1974, when he was arguably at his biggest and best.

In Psalm 90, human life in this world is likened to the life cycle of grass. Here for a season, flourishing then it is soon no more. Baptist preacher C.H. Spurgeon wrote, "Here is the history of the grass- sown, grown, blown, mown, gone: and the history of man is not much more!"

When the Apostle Paul was preaching the gospel in first century Athens to the intelligencia there in the Areopagus, he gave the resurrection of Christ as the proof that there will be a judgement day. The resurrection of Christ and the empty tomb is also the seal of the second advent of Christ. It is the blessed hope because our loved ones who have died in faith are not lost and gone forever.

I Thessalonians 4:13-18, teaches us that when the King returns, He will bring with Him, those "who sleep with Jesus" and we will be reunited with them. The passage above from Philippians 3 teaches us that our lowly bodies, subject to weakness, sickness and sadly death, will be transformed to become like the body of the risen and triumphant Lord's body, no more to suffer weakness, sickness, age and death.

This promise is not for the elite. It is not for the "goody two shoeses" of the world. The promise is to those who acknowledge their sinfulness. Sin is falling short of God's expectations of us. It is overstepping the mark. That is defying God, refusing to submit to His standards, as revealed in the Bible and doing our own sweet thing. In the New Testament, confession literally means "the same words." It is, as we agree with God's verdict of us, that we are sinful and we need to humble ourselves and come to Him for forgiveness, then we are acceptable to Him.

The gospel teaches us that none of us deserve to receive God's mercy and forgiveness, but He gives it to us when we put our trust in Jesus. We cannot boast about it because we did not earn or deserve being made right with God.

Being made right with God, teaches us more about God than it does about ourselves. In the gospels, Jesus is criticised many times by the religious leaders from mixing and eating with people they considered outcasts such as tax collectors, prostitutes and other sinners. Jesus, however told them that He didn't come to call the righteous but sinners to repentance (Matthew 9:13).

We read, in the Epistle to the Hebrews 13:8 that "Jesus Christ is the same, yesterday, today and forever" and receives all who come to Him, just as He did in the New Testament. Religious activities do not make us acceptable to God. The one acceptable to God is the one who cries out, "God be merciful to me, a sinner!"(Luke 18:13).

At the beginning of the chapter, we looked at the 1980 Mr Olympia competition in Sydney when Arnold Schwarzenegger returned to competition after a five-year absence from the stage. That was seen as "the return of the king." As is well documented, when Arnold retired from bodybuilding, he starred in many Hollywood movies. In 1991, he starred in the movie "Terminator II," which was entitled, "Judgement Day!" The New Testament teaches that when the king returns, there will be a Judgement Day.

On this judgement day, all of us will be there to account for the lives we have lived here on earth. Jesus said that on that day, we will even have to "give an account for every idle word" that we speak (Matthew 12:36). That looks bleak for us because we all fall short of God's expectations and transgress His commands. If the truth be told, all of us deserve punishment for our sins. Even people who appear to be outwardly good, virtuous and upstanding citizens. God looks at the heart, below the surface, that part of us unseen by others. But the gospel is good news. Good news because although we are guilty of sin and unworthy to go into the presence of God, we have a Saviour. We have The Saviour, Jesus Christ who took our sins upon Himself on Calvary. C.H.Spurgeon said, "We can stand before God as if we were Christ because Christ stood before God as if He were us!"

Our king, when He returns to judge the earth, receives with joy all those who put their trust in Him. Why would anyone want to be condemned when peace with God is only a prayer away?

In the final chapter, you will read about someone who did just that and came to Him in repentance and pleaded for God's mercy.

6. Mr Universe the Life changer

"I thought this (gospel) was too good to be true. I later found out that it was true!"

As mentioned in the previous chapter, in 1980 the Mr Olympia competition was held at the Sydney Opera House, Sydney, Australia on 4th October. This is the competition where a late entrant was Arnold Schwarzenegger, who, after retiring in 1975 featured in the movie "Pumping Iron", was a surprise competitor. One of the entrants was the Mr America and two times Mr Universe, Dennis Tinerino (he later won another Mr Universe title). He had become a Christian a few years earlier and had gone from an armed robbing, violent, ghetto dwelling, prison serving hoodlum to a preacher. Tinerino toured England and Wales training for the Mr Olympia that year and sharing the gospel whilst there. He writes in his biography of one point during his tour, "When I shared about my newfound faith...I was grieved in my spirit, for there was little or no interest in the things of God. People's hearts seemed as cold as the weather! Nevertheless, we have planted the seed, and...prayed for the people there..."

He may have felt his visit to the UK was a bit futile and fruitless but little did Dennis Tinerino realise that at his seminar at Wulfrun College, Wolverhampton in March 1980, there was a skinny kid from the Whitmore Reans area of the city.

I would like to tell you about my conversion to Christ. Because I was born to Jamaican parents who grew up in 1920's Jamaica, I was dedicated at Waterloo Road Baptist church in Wolverhampton when I was a child. Like most of my generation, I went to Sunday school at a Church of England church around the corner from the house that I was born in. Our mother taught us to say our prayers before we ate and before we went to sleep. If anybody asked me in those days, I would always call myself a Christian. That did not stop me from swearing and from nicking (stealing) things. Amongst the things I had nicked included weights from Aldersley Stadium, the local athletics stadium and home to Wolverhampton and Bilston athletics club. One of the subjects I studied at school, was religious education, even passing my O-level, one of the few in the year to pass the examination, but I never took Christianity seriously and it had little significance to me.

My search for God began in 1980. Because many of my friends and I were skinny during our school days, we began training with weights in 1977. That was the year of the silver jubilee of Queen Elizabeth II and the year Virginia Wade won the Wimbledon women's tennis title (at the time of writing, no other British women has come anywhere near since). It was also the year that my aunt Mavis and Elvis Presley both died (they were born and died the same year). I started training at Aldersley stadium, Wolverhampton, approximately in June of that year, which was roughly a mile from the family home in Evans Street.

My father was a big boxing fan and an avid reader of the "Ring" magazine. I still have many of them in a box, including some from even before I was born when Floyd Patterson was the heavyweight champion of the world. In those magazines, there were the old "Charles Atlas" advertisements about the weedy chap who gets sand kicked in his face at the beach by the big bully in front of a crowd. After this humiliation, the weedy chap goes away, builds up his muscles, developing himself into a "beefcake" then returns to get revenge on the bully. I also saw some of the Joe Weider adverts with many bodybuilding greats of yesteryear such as Dave Draper, Larry Scott, Chuck Sipes, Arnold Schwarzenegger, Franco Columbu, Freddie Ortiz, Rick Wayne and Frank Zane amongst others. These big strong bodybuilders motivated Jasminder Kapur, Shiv Kumar and I to train and get big and strong.

We all wanted to be Mr Universe despite being so skinny! I was also inspired by the "Incredible Hulk" on television which featured Mr America and 1974 Mr Universe winner, big Lou Ferrigno. When I started training, I was roughly 5'10" and 7 stone 10lbs (approximately 49kg or 108 pounds), from memory, skinny but athletic with it. Even though so light, I was by a long way the fastest sprinter in my year at senior school and was a member of Wolverhampton and Bilston athletics club in 1978. I left school in 1979 and carried on training, using Weider muscle shakes or desiccated liver, Emprote plus, Bodybulk or any supplements we could buy at the local health shops in the town centre. The older guys at the gym told us what supplements to use. Thankfully, I was not exposed to anabolic steroids.

In March 1980, Dennis Tinerino came to Wolverhampton to do a seminar on bodybuilding during a tour of the United Kingdom. The seminar was set up in conjunction with Jim Boulton, a teacher at the college who went on to become a successful competitive bodybuilder himself. I went with one of my nephews Michael Phillips (although a nephew, there are 4 years age difference between us) and Jasminder Kapur, mentioned above. At the seminar, Dennis Tinerino was telling us about his bodybuilding career, training and nutrition before fielding questions from those assembled. When the seminar was over, after he had posed on stage, Michael, Jasminder and I went over and had a chat with Tinerino. I remember him telling us that he was a Christian and of its importance because life was short. He related to us how he had been with missionaries in Africa, had seen them pray for the sick and he had witnessed the sick being healed.

When we were leaving the event, I remember Dennis's wife Anita giving Michael the March edition of the Weider Muscle & Fitness magazine because I had already got that one. I remember thinking what nice people they were. In those days, I started reading the Bible daily and started to think about God and the Christian faith. Shiv Kumar, whom I mentioned earlier, used to come round to our house to collect the pools (a betting pool based on predicting the outcome of Division 1 football matches taking place in the week ahead), which our parents marked, hoping to get rich. He wore a necklace with a picture of an Indian Guru named Bhagawan Sri Sathya Sai Baba, or simply Sai Baba on it. I had gone to junior school with Shiv and we were best friends in those days, as he lived at 29 Austin Street and I lived at 67 Evans Street which were very close to each other. Shiv went to the Sai Baba temple in Lonsdale Road, Pennfields, Wolverhampton. He would invite me a few times to the temple and eventually I accepted one of these invitations in the summer of 1980.

I was working at Don Everall on Bilston Road in those days as a trainee coach trimmer (fitting and repairing the interior of passenger coaches). Sai Baba was a miracle working Indian guru with a big international following. Shiv told me that Sai Baba was the rider on the white horse from the Biblical book of Revelation 19:11-16. Sai Baba wore a long red robe (the vesture dipped in blood mentioned in that passage) and he had a big bushy Afro hairstyle (the many crowns on his head). At the temple, I met an electrician named Kishore. At one time, Kishore had been blind and went to India and was healed by Sai Baba after apparently being told by doctors that he would be permanently blind.

Amongst the claims made by Sai Baba were, "I am Jesus, I am Allah, I am Krishna, I am Buddha!" His devotees at the temple taught me that religions are like different paths that lead to the top of the same mountain. One wag (a person who utters wise cracks), a few years back, said to me, "If you are on the mountain and there is more than one path, you are on the wrong mountain!" Shiv told me of one of the devotees who had a dream in which he saw Sai Baba and in this dream, Jesus appeared and came from inside Sai Baba's heart. A photograph of this man and the painting of this dream subsequently appeared in the local evening newspaper, the Express & Star.

I started going with Shiv and his family to the Lonsdale Road temple and even went to temples in Leicester and Wellingborough. At the temple, you saw weird phenomena. This "sacred ash" came out of framed photographs of Sai Baba which were hanging on the temple walls. I saw this in Wolverhampton, Wellingborough and Leicester. Even from photos with glass covering them and with solid walls behind them. One time, we were singing in the Wolverhampton temple and a flower came out of the picture of Sai Baba on the wall. Was that weird or what? The people said that he would often send them pictures from India during their worship in the temple. I could barely believe it! In the temple, there was a book stall from which I purchased a book called, "In defence of Jesus Christ and other Avatars." An avatar, in the Hindu sense, is a manifestation of the gods in the flesh, such as *Krishna*, the god with many arms, *Hanuman*, the monkey god or *Ganesh*, the elephant god. Many of them believe that Jesus Christ is one of the incarnations of Vishnu, the greatest god of the Hindu's. I remember reading the book and one of the things that stuck in my mind was that Christians were described as narrow minded and bigoted, because of the exclusive nature of their faith and at that time I agreed with the sentiments of the book.

In those days, the summer of 1980, I remember walking through West Park, close to where I lived, on a sunny Sunday afternoon with Jasminder Kapur. There was a group of Christians from a local church, Tabernacle Baptist Church from Dunstall Road, holding an open-<u>air</u> service. We stopped and watched. They were performing some of the Biblical narratives, which I thought was fairly entertaining and amusing. I spoke to them when the service was over because I recognised a few of the Caribbean faces from our school days. I recall them saying that going to heaven and being forgiven of your sins was a free gift which cannot be earned or deserved. It was not a matter of keeping the Ten Commandments. I thought that this sounds too good to be true (I later found out that this is true). I accepted some literature from them. I had misunderstood and thought that they meant you could live just anyhow and still go to heaven. I thought to myself, "No wonder people think Christians are hypocrites if they can live as they please." I remember Shiv telling me that a lot of Indians have the mistaken impression that all white people or Westerners are Christians and when they see white people kissing in the streets, drunk or engaging in all manner of rowdy behaviour, they equate this with Christianity. This, along with the days of the Raj, the British Empire and Trans-Atlantic slavery, in the case of my ancestors, has put many people off Christianity, when these doings were perpetrated by Westerners and not true followers of Christ.

Anyway, back to the book, "In Defence of Jesus Christ and Other Avatars." I came to a part in the book which explains why Christians do not believe in Sai Baba. The book quotes from the Gospel of Matthew 24:23-25 where Jesus says, "Then if any man shall say unto you, Lo, Here is Christ, or there; believe it not. For there shall arise false Christs, and false prophets, and shall shew great signs and wonders; insomuch that if it were possible, they would deceive the very elect. Behold, I have told you before." That was it. I thought to myself, "That is very clear, even though this book is defending Sai Baba and co. Here you have Sai Baba saying, 'I'm Jesus, I'm Allah, I'm Krishna, I'm Buddha' and then there's Jesus telling us very clearly that there would be imposters and deceivers trying to deceive God's people!" Those were my thoughts in those days. I was unsettled but remember asking God to guide me.

Not long after that, perhaps a few weeks, my sister Jackie came home from school, she was in the sixth form at Aldersley School, the school I left in 1979. She told me that the Minister from the Baptist church in Dunstall Road had visited the school and invited them to a youth night which was to take place on Friday October 17th 1980. The Minister, Peter Gordon-Roberts, seemed like a good bloke and even cracked a couple of jokes, which appealed to me. I bribed my sister into coming with me because I did not want to go by myself, even though it was only around two hundred yards from where we lived. We duly went along and sat with David and Dennis Ellis, whom we knew from school and from living in Whitmore Reans. I also recognised a few of the faces from the open-air service in West Park a few months earlier on that

Sunday afternoon. I recall being full of questions. That night, there was a group present from B.B.I. (Birmingham Bible Institute). They were explaining the Christian faith and telling us how Jesus had changed their lives and what He meant to them. I remember talking to a chap named Andy and peppering him with questions, "What about Rastas?" "What about Jews?" "What about Hindus?" etc. He was very patient with me and explained that the New Testament was clear and unequivocal. It taught that there was only one way to be saved and that was through Jesus (John 14:6, Acts 4:12 and 1 Timothy 2:5).

I later spoke to an Ulsterman named George Gracie who was there. Although it was a youth night, this man who was in his 70's was still there. He went through a book with me called, "Journey into Life." It explained what a Christian was not. You could go to church, read your Bible and pray without being a Christian. It then explained what a Christian was. It was a person who had come to a point in their life when they realised that they are sinners who needed forgiveness for their sins. I learnt Jesus spoke more about hell than He did about heaven. That night I realised that I was no Christian but was a guilty sinner who needed a Saviour. I said sorry to God and thanked Him that Jesus had paid the penalty which my sins deserved. As I walked home that night, I did not have any visions or see any flashes in the sky, but I felt as though I was where I was supposed to be. It is difficult to fully describe, but it is almost like finding the missing piece of a jigsaw puzzle. The Lord has been refining my person since.

I remember in 1983 that the Lord laid it on my conscience about some weights that I still had at home which I had stolen from Aldersley Stadium in 1978. The Lord made me take them back plus extra. I recall putting them in a blue hessian rucksack and getting onto a bus and going to the club secretary of Wolverhampton and Bilston athletics club's office. The first thing I said to him was, "Do you promise not to call the police?" He said, "Yes." I said to him, "I was a member here a few years ago and I used to steal the weights. I have become a Christian and Jesus has changed my life. Just to show how sorry I am, here are the weights that I had stolen plus some extra ones for the trouble!" The poor chap did not know what to say but I went off home.

Just to clarify my misunderstanding from my encounter with the Christians doing the open-air service in West Park in the summer of 1980. They had told me that receiving eternal life or being forgiven of one's sins is a free gift which cannot be earned or deserved. When I heard that, and discovered that it was not a matter of keeping the Ten Commandments, "going to church", being religious or, in fact, anything you do, my first thoughts were that this is too good to be true. I knew nothing about conversion or the "new birth" also known as being "born again." Being "born again" is not an Americanism but it was Jesus Himself who told a religious leader that unless one is born again, or we may say, converted, they cannot see the Kingdom of God. It is not a matter of turning over a new leaf, or, as the dictionary puts it, "accepting or subscribing to a new set of beliefs." Conversion is more than just head knowledge because we read in James 2:19, "You believe that there is one God. You do well. Even the demons believe-and tremble!" Conversion or being born again is the work of the Holy Spirit on those who are spiritually dead, which is how all human beings enter the world. No matter what country one may be born in, no one is born a Christian. That is why Jesus stresses to Nicodemus the necessity of the new birth. You can read the narrative in the third chapter of the Gospel of John. In John 3:6 Jesus said to Nicodemus, "That which is born of the flesh is flesh." You come out into the world like your parents. They are all sinners, dead to God, and so are we. Jesus sends the Holy Spirit who gives life to a once dead soul.

Over 500 years before Christ, the Old Testament prophet Ezekiel foretold the new birth when he said that God would take out the heart of stone and replace it with a heart of flesh (Ezekiel 11:19). Being born again makes you a new person. We read in 2 Corinthians 5:17, "Therefore, if anyone is in Christ, he is a new creation, old things have passed away; behold, all things have become new." One is given a new life. When a child is born, it is always interesting to see whose characteristics they have. Are they like their mother or father, whose nose, eyes or shaped face do they have? Similarly, when a person is born again or converted, to one extent or another they start to become like their Heavenly Father. They have new desires they did not have before, especially towards the Lord, the Bible and living differently to the way they did previously. For some conversion can feel as though it was a gradual process, as when someone is brought up by godly parents and they cannot necessarily pinpoint the moment they came to Christ, but they know they are spiritually awake. It can also be sudden, as in a Damascus Road experience like Saul of Tarsus. Conversion does have a dramatic effect though and your life will stand out in our modern society.

Christians are not perfect just forgiven. The Lord changes bad people into His children. He gives new life to people who were dead in their trespasses and sins. If He can change me, He can change anybody. Even you. He is the same yesterday, today and forever. That is Jesus Christ, the real Mr Universe.

Artists impression of Dennis Tinerino with me at the age of 17

Even though the book defends Hinduism, it quoted Matthew 24:23-25 where Jesus says, "Then if any man shall say unto you, Lo, Here is Christ, or there; believe it not. For there shall arise false Christs…" This convinced me that Christ was the only way to God.

NOTES

Chapter One

Does God believe in Atheists? John Blanchard (Evangelical Press).

Cited from Hebrews 1:1-3 by Dr John F. MacArthur.

Cited in Evolution booklet by John Blanchard (Evangelical Press).

One Solitary Life- James Allen Francis (1864-1928).

Chapter Two

Cited from bodybuilding documentary *"Pumping Iron"*-Charles Gaines & George Butler.

Antiquities of the Jews- Flavius Josephus.

Ecclesiastical History - Eusebius.

Commentary on Genesis - Origen - Cited by Eusebius

Chapter Three

National Geographic documentary, DNA Mysteries, *"The search for Adam."* Available on YouTube.

Answers in Genesis bulletin editorial Simon Turpin.

Chapter Four

River out of Eden -Richard Dawkins.

The Lion, the Witch and the Wardrobe - C.S. Lewis

The Long Silence - Anonymous.

Chapter Five

The Momentous Event - W.J.Grier

The Treasury of David – C.H.Spurgeon

Gospel Sermon - C.H.Spurgeon

Chapter Six

Supersize your faith - Dennis Tinerino